PERFORMANCE ESSENTIALS

IN THE
Work Place

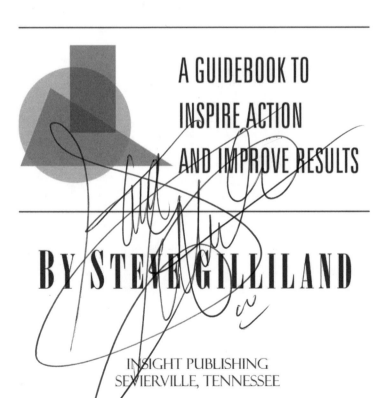

A GUIDEBOOK TO
INSPIRE ACTION
AND IMPROVE RESULTS

BY STEVE GILLILAND

INSIGHT PUBLISHING
SEVIERVILLE, TENNESSEE

Performance
Essentials
in the Work Place

By Steve Gilliland

Published by Insight Publishing Company
P.O. Box 4189
Sevierville, Tennessee 37864

Printed in the United States of America

10 9 8 7 6 5 4 3 2

ISBN: 1-932863-52-4

DEDICATION

This book is affectionately dedicated to my Mother,
Pat Wise.

She influenced my behavior and performance early in life by
instilling a work ethic that has always been my guide in the
workplace.

CONTENTS

ACKNOWLEDGEMENTS

Thanks for this book must be expressed to my parents, Dave and Pat Wise, for providing a home life that was accented with healthy attitudes and Christian principals.

My fourth grade teacher, Paul Reed provided wise counsel in my early years, and a junior high teacher, Bob Lark set an example for positive living in my teen years.

Appreciation is also to be given to my staff at Performance Plus Professional Development for their commitment and support. Michelle Mervos, my oldest son Stephen Gilliland, Amanda Englert, Mike Murray, Chris Procopio, and Joe Varacalli. Their insights, questions and suggestions have helped to guide me in my personal and professional life.

Thank you to my youngest son Josh Gilliland for his incredible work ethic and giving me many stories and illustrations.

Performance Essentials in the Workplace has also been deeply influenced by Bruce Shapiro, a client and friend, whose level of commitment to improving performance in his organization has been an inspiration to me.

Finally, I want to thank Diane, a woman who has shown by example, your performance is only as good as your ability to persevere in any situation. Her unconditional love and support has been an incredible motivation for me. She is, and forever will be, the love of my life.

In memory of Lou Gilliland, my Father,
1932 - 2004

WELCOME

This book was written because I couldn't find another one like it. I have attended many seminars, collected numerous workbooks, and read hundreds of books. Yet everything I have attained doesn't condense the most important pieces of my training, the essentials we need to perform at a high level in the workplace.

As a professional speaker and trainer I have found that most of my clients spend more time talking about how to improve performance in the workplace than about anything else. Through observations, interviews, and past work experience during a twenty-year period, I have gathered practical information on techniques and methods for inspiring action and improving results. It was the absence of any practical and integrated reference material, and repeated requests from many people who attended our seminars, that set me on the long course of putting this book together. Numerous people would request copies of my workbooks and then ask permission to use the material back at their organizations. Of course my philosophy has always been, "share the wealth."

This book is divided into chapters that provide a wealth of information on the five essentials necessary to performance in the workplace. Teamwork, motivation, attitude, organization, and customer service are vital to growth in the workplace, and critical to the survival of some companies. These five essentials are either the organizations' best friends or their worst enemies. They are either intricate parts of the workplace culture, or the missing pieces that keep people and organizations from fulfilling their true mission and vision. These essentials are necessary for sales people, customer relations staff, engineers and scientists, bus drivers, teachers, police officers, nurses, volunteers, high school students, and of course, supervisors, managers and executives in both public and profit-making organizations.

In the pages that follow we will provide you with an overview of each performance essential, numerous quotes to inspire you and your co-workers, and a comprehensive workbook to educate you on these important essentials. The workbook for each section provides a method for you to learn and also a course outline to help train people in your organization. Your company may never achieve its desired culture; however, this book provides the means for doing it with more ease and greater success.

TEAMWORK

Achieving More Together

A diverse group formed each year to compete in a sport is an excellent example of team building. Groups develop into teams when their common purpose is understood by all of the members. Within effective teams each member plays an assigned role using his or her talent to the best advantage. When the members integrate their skills to accentuate strengths and minimize weaknesses, team objectives are usually achieved. When, on the other hand groups play as individuals, they usually fail. Most wins or losses are the result of teamwork. In sports, feedback is often immediate. If teamwork is lacking, good managers can identify where the problems are, and initiate corrective action in order to change things until the desired results are achieved.

Like their athletic counterparts, groups organized to perform business, community and government functions can achieve far more when they work as teams. Unfortunately, many leaders fail to recognize and apply the same principles as they would to coach a sport. In a work organization they do not understand how to transform their group into a productive team. One reason may be that feedback in the form of results is not as quick and dramatic as in athletics. Problems can go unnoticed and corrective action, if taken, can be slow in coming.

Effective teamwork knows no level. It is just as important among top executives as it is among middle managers, first line supervisors or the rank and file. The absence of teamwork at any level (or between levels) will limit organizational effectiveness and can eventually kill an organization. It requires effort to establish and maintain teamwork. If a leader does not place a high value on teamwork it will not occur. Teamwork takes conscious effort to develop and continuous effort to maintain, and the rewards can be great when you begin *achieving more together.*

Commitment is a "no matter what" matter.

TEAM BUILDING BENEFITS

Meet The Demands Of The New Millennium

1. Higher levels of performance
2. Greater customer satisfaction
3. Improved quality, service, and price
4. Pressure to continuously improve and be innovative
5. Increased competitiveness

Seize Opportunities

1. Increase market share
2. Acquire new customers
3. Solve problems by drawing on the talents of a variety of individuals

---

A successful team beats with one heart.

Overcome Challenges

1. Turf battles
2. Decreasing productivity
3. Conflict as a daily occurrence
4. Poor communication
5. Lack of trust and cooperation
6. Mergers or acquisitions
7. Appointment of a new team leader
8. Reorganization or down-sizing
9. New responsibilities with no additional help
10. Apathy

Improves The Organization

1. People
2. Attitude
3. Service
4. Meetings
5. Consistency
6. Communication
7. Creativity
8. Performance

Opportunities multiply when they are seized; they die when neglected.

# # #

TEAM BUILDING MISTAKES

Most Common Mistakes

1. Recruiting
    > Tendency: Hire people for what they know
    > Result: Fire people for who they are

2. Leadership
    > Tendency: Focus on improving systems
    > Result: Doesn't develop people

3. Communication
    > Tendency: Need-to-know basis
    > Result: Confusion

4. Evaluations
    > Tendency: Focus on individual performance
    > Result: No reason to play as a team

5. Compensation
    > Tendency: Based on tenure
    > Result: No incentive to improve

Form A Team For Weak Reasons

1. To lighten the workload of the leader
2. To make workers transfer knowledge to one another to save on training costs
3. To determine the opinions and working styles of the staff
4. To get the staff to work harder

Ten Critical Mistakes

1. Failure to clearly define expectations
2. Failure to establish goals
3. Inattention to training
4. Lack of recognition
5. Failure to provide and receive feedback
6. Lack of involvement
7. Keeping those who don't respond to coaching
8. Permitting negativity to exist
9. Misunderstanding of responsibilities
10. Failure to nurture team building activities

Key Factors That Affect A Team

1. Vision—mission and framework to get results
2. Leadership—effective, capable, and committed
3. Culture—norms that create a climate for excellence
4. Accountability—a way to monitor and improve team processes

---

Do what you value; value what you do.

# # #

TEAM BUILDING CHALLENGES

Changing The Attitude

1. Believing in the mission
2. Creating the expectations
3. Defining accountability
4. Understanding the roles
5. Focusing on individual strengths

Catching The Vision

1. Seeing it
2. Pursuing it
3. Achieving it
4. Helping others see it

Meeting Common Psychological Needs

1. The need to contribute
2. The need to feel competent
3. The need to achieve results
4. The need to be recognized and rewarded

Sustaining The Momentum

1. Trust
2. Enthusiasm
3. Focus
4. Commitment
5. Value

CREATING THE VISION

Provisions

1. Ownership—what we create we support
2. Commitment—helps us see it through at all costs
3. Measurement—insight to see how well we are doing
4. Standard—a context for our decision making
5. Motivation—the reason we do what we do

Process

1. Team member input
   a. Strengths
   b. Weaknesses
   c. Opportunities
   d. Threats
2. Create the objectives—what you will do
3. Design the tactics—how you will do it
4. Determine the resources—what you will need to do it
5. Assign the responsibilities—who will do it

Shared visions are the unifying force of a team.

Goals

1. Specific
2. Measurable
3. Achievable
4. Realistic
5. Timely

Plan

1. Prioritize the objectives
2. Assign deadlines to every tactic
3. Monitor your progress

If you don't like what you're getting—change what you're doing.

# # #

Defining The Process

Accountability

1. Commonality—purpose
2. Expectations—roles
3. Responsibility—ownership
4. Accessibility—availability

Motivation

1. Impact—why we do what we do
2. Contribution—value for what we do
3. Incentive—reward for what we do
4. Deadline—target to finish what we do

Trust

1. Honesty—in every situation
2. Respect—earned
3. Honor—valuing other people
4. Unselfish—putting team first

Integrity

1. Dependability—someone others can count on
2. Flexibility—anticipates and embraces change
3. Adaptability—sensitive to different types of people
4. Reliability—accurate information

DESIGNING THE TEAM

Assess Styles

1. Dominant—tend to be a perfectionist, controlling, arrogant, competitive, focused, and passionate
2. Influential—tend to be persuasive, sociable, self-centered, convincing, charming, and outgoing
3. Balanced—tend to be patient, forgiving, impartial, choosy, restrained, and cautious
4. Loyal—tend to be humble, inflexible, other-centered, sentimental, content, and systematic

Clarify Roles

1. What are your major job responsibilities?
2. What could others do to help you succeed at your job?
3. What could you do to help team members more?
4. Ideally, if you could redesign your job to more fully utilize your potential, minimize the most frustrating parts of your job, or motivate you more, what changes would you make?

People support what they help create.

Deliver Expectations

1. Positive
2. Enthusiastic
3. Responsive
4. Dependable
5. Compatible

Develop Skills

1. Problem solving
2. Communication
3. Organization
4. Creativity

A goal without a deadline is a dream.

# # #

COMMUNICATION ESSENTIALS

Listening

1. Distractions
    a. Personality conflict
    b. Boring content
    c. Vocabulary
    d. Voice quality
    e. Irritating mannerisms
    f. Hygiene and dress
2. Techniques
    a. Assertive position—be open
    b. Eye contact—fight distractions
    c. Take notes—gather information
    d. Listen for "feeling" words—intent vs impact
    e. Never interrupt—withhold judgment
    f. Clarify and verify—paraphrase and reflect

Three Fundamental Factors

1. Be honest and open
2. Feel and show respect
3. Communicate constructively

Delivering Feedback

1. Be informed
2. Be concise
3. Be vulnerable
4. Be focused

Receiving Feedback

1. Focus on the content, not the delivery
2. Remember the goal is long term
3. Control your emotions
4. Take notes
5. Be open to opportunities for improvement
6. Commit to action

Teamwork is lending a hand not pointing a finger.

# # #

PERFORMANCE ESSENTIALS

Team Players—The Qualities

1. Adaptable
2. Committed
3. Disciplined
4. Passionate
5. Positive

Training—The Knowledge

1. Technical skills
2. Soft skills
3. Continuous learning

Coaching—The Leader

1. Understanding—generational emotions and needs
2. Authenticity—revealing mistakes and weaknesses
3. Modeling—matching your actions with your beliefs
4. Attentive—being present for team members

Evaluations—The Plan

1. Periodic assessment in addition to annual review
2. Compensation based on performance, not cost of living
3. Objective, not subjective
4. Focus on developing people first, then the bottom line

MEETING ESSENTIALS

Reason

1. Exchange information
2. Solve problems
3. Brainstorm new ideas
4. Educate
5. Develop plans and programs

People

1. Leader—sets the objective
2. Sponsors—provide the agenda
3. Recorder—records the action plan
4. Timekeeper—monitors agenda
5. Facilitator—runs the meeting

Agenda

1. Objective—clearly defined
2. Discussion items—provided by participants
3. Time limits—discussion items
4. Breaks—preassigned

A meeting with no agenda is like a map with no cities.

Checklist

1. Pre-meeting
   a. Distribute the agenda a few days prior to the meeting
   b. Attach a memo to the agenda that includes the meeting objective, date, time, location, and attendees
   c. Encourage agenda sponsors to plan their parts
   d. Determine the cost
2. Meeting
   a. Begin on time
   b. Keep focused on objective and discussion items
   c. Maintain a parking lot
   d. Develop action plan
      i. Action
      ii. Person responsible
      iii. Deadline
   e. Summarize action plan and pass out meeting evaluation form
   f. Finish on time
3. Post-meeting
   a. Evaluations—returned within 24 hours
   b. Action plan—distribute to attendees within three days

COACHING THE TEAM

Empower

1. Give team members the responsibility to do their job
2. Give team members the authority to make decisions
3. Give team members permission to fail

Delegate

1. Determine what needs to be done—the right thing
2. Determine who should do it—the right person
3. Share why it needs to be done—the importance
4. Share how it needs to be done—the training
5. Share when it needs to be done—the deadline

Brainstorm...someone already has the answer.

Equip

1. Evaluate them—how well can they do?
2. Qualify them—how well will they do?
3. Unite with them—how well can we do together?
4. Invest time in them—how can I personally help them?
5. Provide resources for them—how much better could they be?

Develop

1. Develop self—become a survivor
2. Lead self—become a producer
3. Develop others—become a reproducer
4. Lead others—become a leader

Charisma will get you in the door; credibility will keep you there.

# # #

TRAINING THE TEAM

Provisions

1. If you want confidence, provide encouragement
2. If you want willingness, provide recognition
3. If you want contribution, provide appreciation
4. If you want love, provide acceptance
5. If you want trust, provide honesty
6. If you want goals, provide direction
7. If you want improvement, provide training
8. If you want creativity, provide security

Seminars

1. Performance Plus Professional Development, Inc.—Performanceplus1.com
2. Coloring Outside The Lines, Inc.—ColoringOutsideTheLines.com
3. Ethos Leadership Group—Ethos.com

Audio

1. *"A Treasury Of Motivation"*; Steve Gilliland; Impact Audio
2. *"Do Right";* Lou Holtz; Washington Speakers Bureau
3. *"The Seeds Of Greatness";* Denis Waitley; Nightingale Conant
4. *"Enjoy The Ride";* Steve Gilliland; Impact Audio

Books

1. *The Seven Habits Of Highly Effective People*; Stephen R. Covey; Simon & Schuster
2. *Who Moved My Cheese*; Spencer Johnson, M.D.; Putnam
3. *The 21 Irrefutable Laws Of Leadership*; John C. Maxwell; Thomas Nelson Publishers
4. *Emotional Intelligence*; Daniel Goleman; Bantam Books
5. *Fish!*; John Christensen; Hyperion
6. *Timing Is Everything*; Denis Waitley; Thomas Nelson Publishers
7. *Life Strategies*; Phillip C. McGraw, Ph.D.; Hyperion
8. *The Pursuit Of Wow*; Tom Peters; Vintage Books
9. *High Five*; Don Carew and Eunice Parisi-Carew; Morrow
10. *Enjoy The Ride*; Steve Gilliland; Insight Publishing

If you are in a hole, stop digging.

EVALUATING THE TEAM

Customer Service—Internal And External

1. Works to achieve internal and external customer satisfaction while meeting time, quality, and cost requirements
2. Treats every customer respectfully, courteously, and professionally
3. Keeps things simple and practical
4. Works to improve processes or procedures
5. Doesn't talk negatively about teammates

Teamwork And Attitude

1. Promotes the success of others
2. Supports decisions reached by consensus
3. Communicates clearly
4. Exhibits flexibility and cooperation; willing to switch to other jobs or projects
5. Brings issues and/or conflicts to leadership

If you're all wrapped up in yourself, then you're overdressed.

Company Success

1. Works diligently to achieve desired results
2. Supports team guidelines and procedures
3. Is respectful of coworkers and leaders
4. Makes good use of resources and equipment
5. Responds favorably to required change

Work Habits And Quality

1. Reports to work on time and as scheduled
2. Meets or exceeds standards of quality
3. Works in a safe manner
4. Maintains organized and neat work area
5. Performs work timely with minimal errors

**Integrity is the agreement of our actions
with our beliefs.**

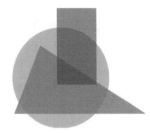

MOTIVATION

Creating Your Edge

I love to tell the story about the chicken and the eagle. It's an old Indian fable about a young brave who took and egg from an eagle's nest and put it in a chicken's nest. When the egg hatched, the eagle thought he was a chicken. As the eagle grew up among the chickens, he learned their way of life. He pecked the ground for food, scratched the dust, and made vocal sounds like the chickens he lived with. One day he looked toward the sky and saw an eagle soaring above him. He flexed his wings and said to his mother, "I wish I could fly like that." "Don't be silly," his mother said, "you're a chicken; only eagles can soar so high in the sky." Feeling foolish and convinced his desire to fly was futile, the eagle went back to scratching and pecking in the dirt. He had, for all practical purposes, become a chicken—because he believed he was a chicken. Never again did he question his role on earth. It is all a matter of perception. When the eagle couldn't fly, it wasn't because he didn't have the natural ability, but rather because his belief was, "I am a chicken, and chickens can't fly." In order to fly, he needed to alter his perception of himself. He had to recognize his God-given abilities, and/or change his mindset concerning these abilities. He had to *believe*! Although our perceptions of reality determine what we believe, what we believe determines what we are and will become. Our *beliefs* determine our *expectations*, our expectations determine our *attitude*, our attitude determines our *behavior,* our behavior determines our *performance,* and our performance determines our *success.* As human beings, we tend to act appropriately to what we believe to be true, regardless of what is actually true or false. In other words, we are a product of conditioning in much the same manner that a computer is the product of its programming. What would you try to accomplish if you knew you wouldn't fail? It is time to change your beliefs about yourself and begin *creating your edge.*

Make your life a mission and never abort it.

ENJOY THE RIDE

Talents To Enjoy The Ride

1. Passion
2. Energy
3. Enthusiasm

Elements To Sustain The Ride

1. Faith keeps you believing
2. Motivation keeps you moving
3. Love keeps you encouraged
4. Courage keeps you exploring
5. Wisdom keeps you safe

Why People Enjoy The Ride

1. Purpose
2. Reward

Why People Don't Enjoy The Ride

Reasons	Solutions
Lack of enthusiasm	Motivation
Boredom	Challenge
Lack of interest	Empowerment
Cling to status quo	Involvement
No innovation	Security
Same thing too long	Development

BELIEVE IN YOURSELF

Roadblocks

1. Low self-expectancy
2. Environment
3. Weak self-image
4. Lack of direction
5. Indecision
6. Lack of follow-through
7. Self-doubt
8. Lack of control
9. Identity awareness
10. Negative self-projection

Defining Your Self-Esteem

1. Never take things personally
2. Never tie yourself to what you can't control
3. Never let anyone decide your worth
4. Never pity or belittle yourself
5. Never compare yourself to others

An adventure is anything beyond your comfort level.

Developing Your Self-Esteem

1. Build on your strengths
2. Acknowledge your weaknesses
3. Make yourself necessary
4. Learn something new every day

Believing In Yourself

1. Self-esteem
2. Patience
3. Perseverance

All motivation is self-motivation.

# # #

LEARN YOUR LIVING

Why We Don't Learn

1. Apathy—the message is never sought
2. Not smart enough—the message doesn't get through
3. Not paying attention—the message sails over our head
4. Not disciplined—the message gets in but not out

Why We Can Learn

1. We have the instructions
2. We have the experience
3. We have the choice

A wish changes nothing. A decision changes everything.

Who Can Help Us Learn

1. Mentor—someone who will teach us, advise us, and show us the way
2. Leader—someone whose excellence can be duplicated
3. Advocate—someone who believes in us

Self-Improvement Resources

1. Books
2. DVDs and Videos
3. Seminars
4. Periodicals

Become an expert in the impossible.

#

Put People First

Two Kinds Of Relationships

1. Instrumental—exists to get something done
2. Social—exists for other reasons
   a. Superficial
   b. Intimate

Ingredients Of A Relationship

1. Love—unconditional
2. Trust—honesty
3. Compassion—sensitivity
4. Commitment—involvement
5. Acceptance—diversity
6. Appreciation—gratitude

Below your means, allows you to realize your dreams.

Communicating In Relationships

1. Don't assume anything
2. Don't accuse
3. Focus on what is right, not who is right
4. Remember their perception is their reality

Building Positive Relationships

1. Value yourself
2. Resolve problems; don't endure them
3. Be who you are and appreciate who they are
4. Be good to your friends to keep them, and to your enemies to convert them
5. Don't judge because they aren't who they should be; pray they become who they could be

---

By chasing "there" you can't appreciate "here."

# # #

VALUE YOUR TIME

Be Accountable For Your Time

1. Plan it
2. Protect it
3. Respect it

Minimize Your Time Wasters

1. Interruptions
2. Lack of planning
3. Internet and email
4. Meetings
5. Disorganization

Maximize Time Savers

1. Schedule your day
2. Delegate
3. Learn to say "no"
4. Over-communicate
5. Utilize peak time

Refocus Your Attention

1. Family
2. Physical well-being
3. Emotional well-being
4. Career

MANAGE YOUR MONEY

The Basic Principles

1. Stick to a budget
    a. Document your spending
    b. Budget all fixed expenses
    c. Keep your budget realistic
    d. Never shop without a list
2. Maximize retirement
    a. Insurance
    b. Investments
    c. Savings
3. Treat savings as a monthly expense
    a. 50% long term—retirement
    b. 30% emergency—the unexpected
    c. 20% emotional—the "wants"
4. Control your debt/income ratio
    a. Have only two credit cards
    b. Only borrow money for mortgage and/or auto loans

Comparison prohibits you from seeing your uniqueness.

# # #

MANAGE YOUR MONEY

Warning Signs—Too Much Credit

1. Only making the minimum payment
2. Balances on credit cards are at the limit
3. Not enough cash to get through the month
4. Borrowing from one source to pay another
5. Worrying about money

Reduce Your Debt

Creditor	Interest	Payment	Balance	Payoff Date
Visa	9.3%	75.00	800.27	04/07/04
Totals				

Budget Your Money

1. **B**uild your credit
2. **U**nderstand your limits
3. **D**ocument your spending
4. **G**et the best deal
5. **E**xpect the unexpected
6. **T**ake action

Motivation has no limits.

# # #

Draw Your Lines

Define Your Lines

1. What lines have I drawn?
2. What are my deadlines?
3. When I reach my lines, what else in my life will improve?
4. What resources do I need to reach my lines?

Draw S.T.R.A.I.G.H.T. Lines

1. **S**pecific
2. **T**imely
3. **R**ealistic
4. **A**ttainable
5. **I**nteresting
6. **G**enuine
7. **H**ealthy
8. **T**raceable

Decide in your mind but choose from your heart.

Reach For Your Lines

1. Compete against yourself
2. Reward yourself
3. Stretch yourself
4. Reassure yourself

Go Above Your Lines

1. Stay focused
2. Make sacrifices
3. Keep on your toes

Desire more than you can accomplish.

# # #

REDEFINE YOUR LUCK

Develop Your Plan

1.   Opportunities
   - a. Discernment to recognize them
   - b. Motivation to act on them
   - c. Determination to seize them
2.   Obstacles
   - a. Courage to confront them
   - b. Strength to overcome them

Be F.A.M.O.U.S. With Your Plan

1.   **F**lexible; be ready for change
2.   **A**daptable; be sensitive to differences
3.   **M**asterful; be extraordinary at something
4.   **O**ptimistic; look for the positive in everything
5.   **U**nselfish; give more than you take
6.   **S**teadfast; stay committed to the plan

Be Open To All Possibilities

1.   Strive for perfection—don't plan for mediocrity
2.   Push the limit—you get 0% of what you don't pursue
3.   Risk success—don't fail by never trying

Match Your Habits To Your Plan

1.   Destructive
2.   Constructive

COMMIT TO ACTION

Action Requires Discipline

1. Hard work
2. Stamina
3. Character

Discipline Requires Commitment

1. Interest—you only do things when it is convenient
2. Vow—is an obligation; you accept no excuses, only results

Commitment Requires Initiative

1. Initiative is not what we think
2. Initiative is not what we know
3. Initiative is not what we believe
4. Initiative is not what we say
5. Initiative is what we do

Enjoying the ride makes success priceless.

Initiative Requires Action

1. Start the process: don't fear what you want the most
2. Unlock your potential: give up what you are to receive what you can become
3. Create your own reality: dare to be different
4. Choose your attitude: no one can ruin your day without your permission
5. Expect challenges: a path with no problems leads nowhere
6. Show up every day: always perform at your highest level
7. Stay in the game: success stops when you do

Motivation is going ahead without success.

# # #

PUNCTUATE THE POSITIVE

Your Attitude Is Everything

1. The librarian of your past
2. The speaker of your present
3. The prophet of your future

Your Attitude Reveals Your Response

1. Negative
    a. Pessimistic
        i. Distorts the picture
        ii. "What if" belief system
    b. Unrealistic
        i. Reactive to problems
        ii. Takes on everything; accomplishes nothing
        iii. Expects something for nothing
2. Positive
    a. Optimistic
        i. Sees the bigger picture
        ii. "I can" belief system
    b. Realistic
        i. Anticipates obstacles
        ii. Understands limitations
        iii. Improves continuously

Factors That Influence Your Attitude

1. Past mistakes
2. Present circumstances
3. Future fears
4. Unforeseen problems
5. Relationships
6. Change

Your Intake Affects Your Outlook

1. What we read
2. What we watch
3. What we hear
4. Who we're with

Every little quit hurts.

# # #

VISUALIZE TO REALIZE

Risk Being First

1. Courage
2. Confidence
3. Creativity

Prepare To See The Horizon

1. Glasses—correct your vision
2. Binoculars—bring your vision closer
3. Windshield Wipers—clear the obstruction from your vision
4. Microscope—see below the surface of your vision
5. Flashlight—enlighten your vision
6. Sunglasses—remove the glare from your vision

Every day is a gift from God, that's why it's called the present.

See Beyond The Horizon

1. If you don't know, go find out
2. When you make a mistake, admit it
3. Don't avoid problems, go through them
4. Don't make promises, make commitments
5. Never be content with how good you are
6. Learn from those who are superior
7. Always look for a better way to do it

Move Beyond Your Comfort Zone

1. Discover more
2. Learn more
3. Affirm more

Extraordinary people JUST over DO IT.

\# \# \#

REFUSE TO QUIT

Acknowledge Your Feelings

1. Realize quitting is a natural feeling
2. It's okay to express your feelings
3. Don't give in to the feelings of quitting
4. Base your feelings on today
5. Ignore those who try to influence your feelings negatively
6. Your feelings are unique to your situations

Control Your Decisions

1. Never make any decision when you are experiencing a shift in emotion
2. Recruit others to help make your decisions
3. Always remember quitting is a permanent decision

Flexibility is when "what is" evolves immediately into "what was."

Embrace Your Adversity

1. Learn from it
2. Grow because of it
3. Change as a result of it

Remember Your Mentors

1. Fred Astaire

After his first screen test in 1933, MGM testing director said, "Can't act. Slightly bald. Can dance a little."

2. Vince Lombardi

An expert said, "He possesses minimal football knowledge. Lacks motivation."

3. Walt Disney

Was fired by a newspaper for lacking ideas. He also went bankrupt several times.

4. Ludwig Beethoven

His teacher called him a hopeless composer.

Growth is the process of failing to ultimately succeed.

# # #

ATTITUDE

Dealing With Negativity

Most of us are so geared towards the negatives of life that we agree with George Carlin, the comedian, who jokes, "Positive thinking is miscalculation." We come to believe that surely the world was not organized for good. We convince ourselves that it was not organized for *our* good. Those who believe the world was capitulated to evil naturally believe it would be a miscalculation to anticipate good for *themselves*.

Positive thinking is not miscalculation. I've found it to be the way life works best. Positive thinking is more important to us than we know. Dr. Norman Vincent Peale once pointed out that it takes ten positives to overcome one negative. We need as many positives in our lives as we can get! When we begin to look beyond our personal scars and focus on our stars, we find we are starting to think and act positively. I've discovered that when I can be positive, even toward negative situations, positive results occur. Positive results, of course, move us forward. Positive thinking about our goals, our dreams, our aspirations helps us to go for the max and live a more fulfilling life.

Call this philosophy anything you choose. Call it *positive thinking, possibility thinking*, or a *positive mental attitude*. Whatever term we choose, it means thinking, acting, and reacting *affirmatively*. It means thinking positively in love and faith, not negatively in fear and distrust of other people, circumstances, happenings, and life events. In order to deal with negativity we must begin with ourselves. Easy to say, but I've found I really have to work at it. Negativity is all around us. I find I must focus my thoughts towards healthy, positive ends. It's easy to talk the talk, hard to walk the walk. Meanwhile, I try to fast from negativity and practice a positive approach to my challenges. I've found that positive thinking really works when *dealing with negativity*.

Positive action always brings positive results.

DEFINING NEGATIVITY

Where It Begins—Childhood

1. Abandonment—feeling unwanted
2. No stability—irresponsibility
3. No limits—inability to say "no"
4. Avoidance—need to be liked outweighs need to confront
5. Discipline—control or out of control
6. Attention—need excitement, chaos, or drama

How It Occurs—Contradictory Expectations

1.	Taking risks	Being correct
2.	Being decisive	Being participative
3.	Being ambitious	Being loyal to a company
4.	Taking charge	Being a team player
5.	Personal goals	Organizational goals

Enthusiasm makes everything different.

Why It Continues

1. Habitual thinking makes it normal to focus on wrong
2. Cultures accept it
3. We tolerate it
4. It sells—sensationalism
5. It naively elevates self-esteem
6. It subtly gets in
7. It gets attention

What It Costs

1. Productivity
   a. Substandard performance
   b. Morale
   c. Deadlines aren't met
2. Quality
   a. Mistakes increase
   b. Average is accepted
   c. Confidence is lost
3. Wasted resources
   a. People—potential
   b. Time
   c. Money

# # #

UNDERSTANDING HUMAN BEHAVIOR

How We Get The Way We Are

1. Biology
   a. Genetics
   b. Present physiological characteristics
2. Environment
   a. Caught and taught behaviors
   b. Parents or parental figures
   c. Role models, friends, and idols
   d. Cultural conditioning
   e. Societal values
   f. Training and education
   g. Experiences
   h. Circumstances (past and present)
3. Personal choices
   a. Behaviors, decisions, and beliefs
   b. Constructive choices—responsible and helpful
   c. Destructive choices—irresponsible and harmful

Replace all negatives with positives.

The Behavioral Chain Reaction

1. Stimuli
2. Thoughts
3. Actions
4. Habits
5. Character
6. Life Path

Changing Human Behavior

1. Willingness to learn and grow
2. Awareness of the need for change
3. Incentive to change
4. Commitment to change
5. Realistic plan for change
6. Support and encouragement
7. Accountability
8. Constructive feedback on progress
9. Opportunity to learn from mistakes
10. Reasonable consequences for continued noncompliance

Attitudes are contagious. Be a carrier.

Helping Others To Change

1.   Care—show you have a genuine desire to be helpful
2.   Make aware—discuss the issues openly and honestly
3.   Understand—listen and understand without condoning or judging
4.   Reason—evaluate present choices and possible constructive alternatives and the consequences of continuing old behavior
5.   Develop commitment to change—explore what a person is willing to own responsibility for doing

Avoid Negative Stimuli

1.   Relationships
2.   Information

Refocus Your Attention

1.   Important
2.   Urgent

Problem solving starts with a positive outlook.

Value Other People

1. Have an attitude of genuine caring
2. Actively listen and demonstrate interest
3. Focus on problems, not people
4. Be honest
5. Assume the best about people
6. Practice patience and self-control
7. Constructively express your feelings

Pursue The Positive

1. Maintain a childlike innocence
2. Accept life on life's terms
3. Guard your self-talk
4. Burn your bridges
5. Make a difference

Attitude doesn't solve problems, it only determines the outcome.

IDENTIFYING NEGATIVE BEHAVIOR

Unrealistic

1. Perfectionist
    a. Identifying Feature: Lack of tolerance and patience
    b. Root Cause: Insecure
2. Procrastinator
    a. Identifying Feature: Overwhelmed
    b. Root Cause: Disorganized
3. Workaholic
    a. Identifying Feature: Career is #1 priority
    b. Root Cause: Fear of losing control

Undisciplined

1. Spoiled
    a. Identifying Feature: Nothing is ever good enough
    b. Root Cause: Discontent
2. Autonomous
    a. Identifying Feature: Never takes responsibility
    b. Root Cause: Not afraid of consequences
3. Coddled
    a. Identifying Feature: Repeat same mistakes
    b. Root Cause: No consequences

Identifying Negative Behavior

Disruptive

1. Cynics
    a. Identifying Feature: Nothing will ever work
    b. Root Cause: Not empowered
2. Instigators
    a. Identifying Feature: Gossiping and positioning
    b. Root Cause: Lack self-confidence
3. Whiners
    a. Identifying Feature: Chronic complaining
    b. Root Cause: Seeking attention

Dormant

1. Resisters
    a. Identifying Feature: Likes status quo
    b. Root Cause: Never had to change
2. Compromiser
    a. Identifying Feature: Settles for less
    b. Root Cause: Lacks self-esteem
3. Apathetic
    a. Identifying Feature: Doesn't care
    b. Root Cause: Sees no value

RESPONDING TO NEGATIVE BEHAVIORS

Unrealistic

1. Perfectionist
   a. Reassure them
   b. Recognize them
2. Procrastinator
   a. Don't give them more than they can handle
   b. Assign deadlines
3. Workaholic
   a. Don't compromise your own priorities
   b. Encourage family and leisure time

Undisciplined

1. Spoiled
   a. Don't give in to their wants
   b. Reason with reality
2. Autonomous
   a. Hold them accountable
   b. Provide support and encouragement
3. Coddled
   a. Communicate the impact
   b. Explain possible consequences

Anger is only one letter short of danger.

Disruptive

1. Cynics
    a. Make them part of the process
    b. Give them permission to fail
2. Instigators
    a. Refuse to tolerate
    b. Confront
3. Whiners
    a. Don't give in or join in
    b. Make them feel valued

Dormant

1. Resisters
    a. Show them the benefits
    b. Help them to visualize the end result
2. Compromiser
    a. Challenge them
    b. Encourage them
3. Apathetic
    a. Provide a reason to care
    b. Show them you care

Doubt your doubts, not your beliefs.

# # #

INFLUENCING NEGATIVE BEHAVIOR

Cultivate Richer Relationships

1. Be vulnerable—admit your fears and shortcomings
2. Stop making negative assumptions
3. Stop being so critical
4. Get more involved—care enough to know, know enough to care
5. Be willing to change first

Practice Being Agreeable

1. Apologize when appropriate
2. Be willing to talk about issues
3. Acknowledge their viewpoint
4. Recognize good points

Be Open To Their Thoughts And Feelings

1. Always be fair and equitable
2. Practice participation, not dictation
3. Think of what they want
4. Respect their perception
5. Don't argue your opinion

Set The Right Example

1. Always deal with the facts
2. Practice being outstanding
3. Communicate openly and honestly
4. Match your actions to your beliefs

DEFUSING ANGER

The Source Of Anger

1. Activating event—something is altered or changed
2. Belief system—the alteration or change is opposite our conviction or opinion
3. Response system—our biological, environmental, and personal choices we have been imprinted with trigger us
4. Consequence—depending on the consequence if any, determine our willingness and degree of response

Calming Techniques

1. Value their opinion
2. Anticipate their emotion
3. Nurture their ego
4. Transfer their energy

Enough white lies will make you go color blind.

Reduce Defensiveness

1. Listen
2. Avoid the A.D.R. cycle
   a. Accuse
   b. Defend
   c. Re-accuse
3. Offer suggestions rather than disagreeing
4. Mirror their feeling

Use Tact

1. **T**alk
2. **A**fter
3. **C**areful
4. **T**hinking

Keep your heart right even when it is sorely wounded.

# # #

RESOLVING CONFLICT

Reasons For Conflict

1. Personality differences
2. Organizational culture
3. Values
4. Goals
5. Job descriptions
6. Perception
7. Communication
8. Baggage
9. Policies and procedures
10. Available resources

Conflict Can Be Positive

1. Enhances relationships
2. Increases productivity
3. Promotes growth and learning
4. Achieves goals

Love is forgiving; commitment is forgetting.

Conflict Styles

1. Avoidance
2. Accommodation
3. Compromise
4. Dominate
5. Collaboration

Confront Assertively

1. Express your feelings
2. Communicate the impact
3. Validate the concern
4. Ask for solutions
5. Agree on a direction
6. Deliver the consequences
7. Commit to the individual

Attitude is accepting and embracing life's challenges.

# # #

COPING ESSENTIALS

Patience

1. Control your emotions during a confrontation
2. Make decisions based on accurate and complete information and not solely on the opinions of others
3. Do not deliver ultimatums prematurely whenever a problem arises in an effort to solve it quickly

Awareness

1. Don't ignore the problem hoping it will eventually go away
2. Don't assume the problem is an isolated occurrence

Consistency

1. Focus on problems, not personalities
2. Confront in private
3. Be sure your motive is honorable

Communication

1. Listen to their side of the issue
2. Don't make assumptions regarding their feelings
3. Ask them instead of telling them
4. Focus on what is right, not who is right

# # #

REDUCING STRESS

Stress-Producing Behaviors

1. Complaining—nothing is ever right
2. Indecisive—can't make decisions
3. Inflexible—rejecting anything new
4. Couching—always sitting at home, tending to be fatigued, and pulse rate increases
5. Disorganization—"so what" attitude
6. Self-centered—rebellious and can't handle criticism
7. Scapegoat—blaming others or circumstances for your problems
8. Apathetic—playing the role of the victim
9. Impatient—it has to be now
10. Overindulgence—too much eating, drinking, smoking, or any other stimuli that can be destructive if not moderated

Most Common Stress-Producing Circumstances

1. Perfectionism—every responsibility has to be perfect and completed
2. Guilt—you aren't meeting the expectations of others
3. Change—you fear the outcome
4. Relationships—you anticipate unpleasant encounters and/or conflict
5. Finances—too much debt and not enough money
6. Job—inconsistent workload, unclear expectations, monotonous tasks, inadequate communication and leadership

Checklist To Reduce Stress

1. Go to bed early—become a morning person
2. Eat a well-balanced diet—stay energized
3. Take a walk—maintain your metabolism
4. Spend ten minutes of quiet time—reboot your brain
5. Take your breaks and lunch hours—don't cheat yourself
6. Do something fun—play
7. Try something new—learn to let go
8. Set limits—learn to say "no"
9. Go home on time—never forget what's important
10. Have a support person—keep encouraged

Keys To Handle Stress

1. Identify your stressors—handle the truth
2. Minimize your stressors—life rewards action
3. Assign the right value to circumstances
4. Be honest in everything

Success is being happy, not right.

# # #

KEEPING BALANCE

Internal Balance

1. Mental
2. Emotional
3. Physical
4. Spiritual

External Balance

1. Family
2. Work
3. Play
4. Relationships
5. Social life
6. Financial
7. Activities

When the past tries to dominate your thoughts, let your dreams ignite your day.

Internal Resources

1. Expose your mind to constructive inputs
2. Willingness to know, process, and express your feelings rationally and constructively
3. Physical fitness
    a. Exercise
    b. Diet
4. Loving others and self in the harmony in your life combined with the depth of your wisdom and correctness of your beliefs

External Resources

1. Loving unconditionally
2. Loving what you do, why you do it, and who you do it with
3. Taking time to have fun
4. Loving like you have never been hurt
5. Dancing like no one is watching
6. Realizing abundance is the result of appreciation, not accumulation
7. Learning how to relax

You will never leave where you are until you decide where you would rather be.

# # #

CHANGING YOUR PATH

Stimuli

1. Internal things that cause a response
2. External things that cause a response

Response

1. Thoughts—interact with our emotional and physical system to produce actions. Constructive thoughts lead to constructive actions.
   In this context, *constructive* means responsible, self-developing, and mature. The word *destructive* means irresponsible, self-defeating, and immature.

2. Actions—tend to be consistent with our thoughts. Inconsistencies may be controlled by subconscious thoughts, our emotions, or our physical system and tend to result in inner tension. Actions that are practiced become habits. Constructive actions lead to constructive habits.

Your day goes the way the corners of your mouth go.

Consequences

1. Habits—practiced thoughts, feelings, and actions. Our habits shape our character. Constructive habits lead to the development of a healthy, strong character.

2. Character—our mental, emotional, physical, and spiritual characteristics as a whole person. Our character shapes our life path.

3. Life Path—long-term behavioral patterns, our life style (including our priorities, goals, and activities), and our destiny as a winner or loser. A change in character will produce a change in our life path by affecting our behavioral patterns, life style, or destiny.

End Results

Our responses and the constructive, destructive, or neutral consequences that they may have on our habits, character, and life path result in outcomes that may affect future stimuli or responses.

Extraordinary people discuss ideas, ordinary people discuss events, and shallow people discuss people.

ORGANIZATION

Managing Multiple Priorities

A s far back as the early 1900s, Victor Pareto explained why a priority system was so important in securing effectiveness. His rule, when applied to setting priorities, states that 80 percent of the value of a group of items is generally concentrated in only 20 percent of the items. In other words, you can be 80 percent effective by achieving 20 percent of your goals. If you have a daily action list of ten items, you can expect to be 80 percent effective by successfully completing only the two most important items on the list. To be effective you must concentrate on the most important items. You must make a commitment to focus on true priority items.

At the beginning of every day, I rank the five most important things I have to do. Then I go to work on number one, and continue to work until I am finished. When I finish the first task, I reevaluate the other four items to make sure nothing has changed in the ranking. I then go to work on number two. When it's done, I reevaluate, and then work on number three. If the day ends and I haven't finished all five, I never worry. I wouldn't have got all five done using any other method, either. And, I did, in fact, do the most important thing on my list (which today was writing this chapter).

Even if the day goes by and I don't even finish number one, I always remind myself that I was still working on the most important thing. The secret is to choose what's most important to you and do it first. It's that simple. The hard part is deciding what is most important. Goethe said, "Things which matter most must never be at the mercy of things which matter least." E.M. Gray spent his life searching for the one common denominator that all successful people share. He found it wasn't hard work, good luck, or astute human relations, though those were all important. The one factor that seemed to transcend all the rest was putting first things first to be successful at *managing multiple priorities.*

Abundance is a result of appreciation not accumulation.

MANAGING YOUR PURPOSE

Define Your Purpose

1. Goals
2. Plan
3. Rewards

Define Yourself

1. Self-acceptance
2. Self-esteem
3. Self-respect
4. Self-pleasing

Create Your Own Reality

1. No one can ruin your day without your permission
2. Decide to be happy
3. Success stops when you do
4. When your ship comes in, be willing to unload it
5. Give life's precious moments value—share them
6. Don't fear what you want the most
7. Make yesterday the deadline for all complaints
8. Look for opportunities, not guarantees
9. Make now the most interesting time of all
10. When things go wrong, don't go with them

Focus On N.O.W.

1. **N**ever look back
2. **O**thers can't stop you
3. **W**e will never have it all together

MANAGING YOUR ATTITUDE

Concerning Change

1. Awareness—your ability to identify issues and behaviors that need to be changed
2. Acknowledgment—admitting you need to make a change
3. Willingness—the ability to move from believing you should change to desiring and choosing to change
4. Strategy—the tactical plan to deliver the change
5. Accountability—a person who will hold you to changing and monitor your progress
6. Perseverance—your ability to hold on

Concerning Forgiveness

1. Toward yourself
   a. What was your intent
   b. What will you do differently the next time
   c. Move forward and don't look back
2. Toward others
   a. Allow yourself to express your feelings
   b. Examine their intent—look beyond the impact
   c. Be compassionate—care
   d. Move forward and don't look back

A "will be" is a "has been" in progress.

Concerning Failure

1. Welcome the lessons - they precede success
2. Focus on your strengths
3. Acknowledge your limitations
4. Cancel your "pity parties"

Concerning The Future

1. Stimuli
   a. External
   b. Internal
2. Responses
   a. Thoughts
   b. Actions
3. Consequences
   a. Habits
   b. Character
   c. Life Path

Never complain about what you permit.

\# \# \#

Managing Your Stress

Five Ways To Combat Job Stress

1. Don't react, act—Identify the underlying issue. Try to stay objective, especially if other people are involved. Use friends, trusted co-workers and others who may have a valuable perspective to help analyze the situation and identify the basic issues.

2. Take control—Again, use carefully selected friends and co-workers to help define and reinforce the course of action. The key is to do something.

3. Learn effective communication skills
   a. Organize thoughts and key points
   b. Express ideas clearly and logically
   c. Objectively identify the fundamental stress issues
   d. Identify a solution or course of action
   e. Identify the benefits to your superior and the company

4. Create a means to combat boredom—Learn why your job is necessary, how it contributes to the company's overall growth and quality of the products.

5. Know what you like about your job—Figure out how to involve yourself in those aspects, either by volunteering for additional responsibilities, seeking additional training or transferring to another department. If you don't like anything about the job, consider changing jobs.

Take Charge

1. Implement a stress-free diet

      a. Eat foods that will combat stress such as citrus fruits or other sources of vitamin C

      b. Avoid foods that aggravate stress such as deep-fried foods high in fat

2. Manage stress through relaxation

3. Work out stress through exercise

Balance Career And Family

1. Decide what's important—You have to agree on work and home priorities, both individually and as a family. This will, no doubt, involve making difficult choices, many of which involve money.

2. Set limits—You can't do it all and neither can your partner. So set limits and discuss them so that expectations are realistic.

3. Learn when to say "no"—Say "no" when a request or demand is made that conflicts with priorities or exceeds limits that have been set.

4. Don't give in to guilt—If you've defined priorities and limits objectively and are willing to stay flexible and cooperative with your partner, there is no reason to feel guilty.

Combat Financial Stress

1. Check your priorities and expectations—Are you trying to create an unrealistic (and unaffordable) lifestyle? Why?

2. Establish a budget—If you can create a balanced budget, it becomes an impartial means for settling future spending disputes. (The budget, not individual preferences or impulse, then dictates spending decisions.)

3. Create a savings program—Having money tucked away is insurance against future financial stress should a job loss, emergency, illness or home repair occur.

Anytime you spend time doing something someone else can do; you won't have time to do what only you can do.

MANAGING YOUR RELATIONSHIPS

Through Love

1. Acceptance
2. Support
3. Patience
4. Unconditional

Through Trust

1. Honesty
2. Integrity
3. Respect
4. Honor

Through Appreciation

1. Appreciate their interests
2. Appreciate their differences
3. Appreciate their contributions
4. Appreciate their efforts

Through Focus

1. On "what" is right
2. Not on "who" is right

Become addicted to continuous self-improvement.

Internal Balance

1. Mental
2. Emotional
3. Physical
4. Spiritual

External Balance

1. Family
2. Work
3. Play
4. Relationships
5. Social life
6. Financial
7. Activities

Clarity is the perspective you can't see.

Internal Resources

1. Expose your mind to constructive inputs
2. Willingness to know, process, and express your feelings rationally and constructively
3. Physical fitness
    a. Exercise
    b. Diet
4. Loving others and self in the harmony in your life combined with the depth of your wisdom and correctness of your beliefs

External Resources

1. Loving unconditionally
2. Loving what you do, why you do it, and who you do it with
3. Taking time to have fun
4. Loving like you have never been hurt
5. Dancing like no one is watching
6. Realizing abundance is the result of appreciation, not accumulation
7. Learning how to relax

The important thing is to keep the important thing the important thing.

# # #

Managing Your Activities

Value Your Time

1. Schedule it—take 15 minutes to plan your day
2. Maximize it—identify your peak productivity time
3. Respect it—reduce time wasters
4. Protect it—utilize time savers

Reduce Time Wasters

1. Interruptions—telephone and drop-in visitors
2. Lack of goals and planning
3. Message retrieval—voice mail and email
4. Meetings
5. Disorganization
6. Internet
7. Bureaucracy—peers and boss
8. Lack of self-discipline
9. Television
10. Crisis management

Courage is being scared and then doing the thing you think you can't do.

Utilize Time Savers

1. Plan your day
2. Delegate
3. Learn to say "no"
4. Never assume
5. Maximize your peak time

End Procrastination

11. Recognize you have a problem
12. Do something—it's better than nothing
13. Break tasks into small action steps
14. Set a deadline
15. Avoid perfectionism
16. Avoid over-commitment
17. Do it now

Elevation is the act of reaching down.

# # #

MANAGING YOUR SPACE

Inventory—One Space At A Time

1. Personal—home
   a. Storage
      i. Closets
      ii. Garage
      iii. Attic
      iv. Basement
   b. Functional
      i. Cabinets
      ii. Drawers
   c. Display—countertops
2. Professional—work
   a. Essential—desk
   b. Interactive—credenza and office file cabinets
   c. Destination—storage file cabinets and shelves

Retention Plan—Space

1. Design it
2. Use appropriate containers
3. Make it easily accessible

Relocation Plan—Stuff

1. Discard it
2. Donate it
   a. Salvation Army
   b. Goodwill
   c. Local shelter
3. Pass it on
   a. Family
   b. Friends
4. Sell it
5. Cancel it
   a. Unnecessary subscriptions
   b. Memberships
6. File it

The Keys

1. Inventory from the outside in
2. Implement a replacement strategy
3. File all paper

Follow the talent you have been given.

\# \# \#

Managing Your Files

Action Files

1. To Tickler
2. To Route
3. To Read
4. To File

Tickler Files

1. Daily—1 to 31
2. Miscellaneous—January to December

To manage priorities, you must first know what they are.

Interactive Filing Systems

1. Alphabetic
2. Numeric
3. Subject
   a. Dictionary
   b. Encyclopedic
      i. Primary—file guides
      ii. Secondary—hanging file folders
      iii. Tertiary—file folders

Finding The Lost File

1. Look in files immediately in front of or behind the original correct location
2. Look between files
3. Look in the bottom of the file drawer
4. Check in, on, or around the copying and fax machines
5. Check in the break room or coffee area
6. Email coworkers
7. Check the "office pack rats" work area

Give some people an inch and they think they're a ruler.

# # #

Managing Your Papers

Leave Nothing "Homeless"

1. Trash it
2. File it
3. Purge it

Handling Incoming Mail

1. If possible, assign a person to sort through your mail, weeding out any junk mail that you still are receiving
2. Process your mail at the same time each day—standing
3. Get your name off of mailing lists
4. Direct Mail Association
5. Credit Bureau Association
6. Bureaus "opt out"
7. Don't open it if your name is misspelled or your title is wrong
8. File it or trash it

Give without remembering; receive without forgetting.

Handling Incoming Correspondence

1. Move your incoming tray off of your desk—get it out of your line of sight
2. Process your incoming tray twice daily—standing
3. File it or trash it
4. Have the necessary support pieces in close proximity to your incoming tray
   a. Waste basket
   b. Action files
   c. Miscellaneous tickler files

Paper Items That Bury Your Desk

1. Items you need to act on
2. Items someone else needs to act on
3. Items of interest
4. Items that need to be filed
5. Items you don't know what to do with
6. Items that are useless

I would rather see a sermon than hear one.

# # #

MANAGING YOUR TECHNOLOGY

Fax Machine

1. Your fax machine should be programmable and provide you with clear copies
2. Position it in close proximity to your incoming correspondence tray
3. Educate personnel on usage regarding incoming and outgoing faxes
4. Check your fax machine only during scheduled intervals and, if possible, have someone place your faxes in your incoming tray—don't stand by it

Voice Mail

1. When you leave or respond to a message, you should outline your main points prior to leaving the message
2. Introduce yourself and state your objective
3. Educate your colleagues that you check your voice mail daily at regular designated times (maximum of three)
4. Be clear, concise, state all numbers slowly, and repeat numbers
5. If a response is required, let them know when you're available
6. You should have specific instructions on your voice mail outlining how a person can transfer to someone else for immediate action
7. Your voice mail system should have a capacity to hold only ten 90-second messages

Email

1. Create an email policy and enforce it

2. Hardware/software databases are proprietary, which reinforces why there should be no personal usage

3. Audit the database every six months

4. Include the policy in the handbook and explain the penalty for violations

5. Determine how you want them to respond

6. Don't let email linger in your mailbox—read it, act on anything that you can handle immediately in two minutes or less, file it, or delete it as soon as possible

7. Set up two action folders for items requiring more than two minutes of focused attention: "Read" folder and "Reply" folder

8. Don't cc everyone in the company—the more you send, the more you receive

9. When replying, omit the original text—if the sender can't remember the original message, how important was it?

10. Avoid the routine email—thank you notes and FYI

11. Be responsible—never send a message you wouldn't want to receive yourself or one that you wouldn't want your supervisor to see

12. Turn off the indicator—only check your email at designated times—maximum of three

13. Keep the messages short—use the subject line and attach documents

Internet

1. Monitor—communicate and specify scope and frequency
2. Limit personal use to before work, after work, or during lunch
3. Outline disciplinary action in detail
4. Block inappropriate site access

If you do not believe in yourself, very few other people will.

# # #

MANAGING YOUR MEETINGS

Reason

1. Exchange information
2. Solve problems
3. Brainstorm new ideas
4. Educate
5. Develop plans and programs

People

1. Leader
2. Facilitator
3. Recorder
4. Time Keeper
5. Participants

Agenda

1. Objective—clearly defined
2. Discussion items—provided by participants
3. Time limits—discussion items
4. Breaks—preassigned

If you fail to plan, you're planning to fail.

Checklist

1. Pre-meeting
   a. Distribute agenda a few days prior to the meeting
   b. Attach a memo to the agenda that includes the meeting objective, date, time, location, and attendees
   c. Encourage agenda sponsors to plan their parts
   d. Determine the cost
2. Meeting
   a. Begin on time
   b. Keep focused on objective and discussion items
   c. Maintain a parking lot
   d. Develop action plan
      i. Action
      ii. Person responsible
      iii. Deadline
   e. Summarize action plan and pass out meeting evaluation form
   f. Finish on time
3. Post-meeting
   a. Evaluations—returned within 24 hours
   b. Action plan—distribute to attendees within three days

MANAGING YOUR PLAN

Commit To Making Necessary Changes

1. Purpose _____
2. Attitude _____
3. Stress _____
4. Relationships_____
5. Responsibilities_____
6. Activities _____
7. Space _____
8. Files _____
9. Paper _____
10. Technology _____
11. Meetings _____
12. Plan to fill in the above eleven and make the commitment

Keys To Making Changes

1. Write them down—give them to a friend in an envelope
2. Establish deadlines
3. Monitor your progress—know your partners
4. Make yourself accountable—have a friend mail the changes to you in six months
5. Write down the potential obstacles—what might get worse
6. Make a list of the resources necessary to make the changes—utilize the resources you have

Life-Balancing Questions

1. What part of your internal balance needs improvement?

2. What part of your external balance needs improvement?

3. Do your actions match your answers?

Life-Balancing Benefits

1. Richer relationships
2. Longer life
3. Happiness
4. Enjoyment
5. Inner peace

If you want to be respected, you have to like what you see in the mirror.

# # #

CUSTOMER SERVICE

Serving 2 Succeed

A true customer focus, a true service focus, requires a fundamental re-learning process that goes to the deepest levels of the organizational culture. It requires an open and honest effort to discern the truth of customer value and determination to implement it in a very thorough way.

All of us still have much to learn if we are to move our organizations beyond the level of slogans and platitudes about customer service. Nearly two decades after the publication of Service America!, which launched a so-called service revolution in the USA and eventually abroad, can we really say most of our businesses, hospitals, and schools are truly customer-focused? Just consult your own recent experience and you'll see that most of the real opportunities still lie before us.

No matter what you sell—products, services, or a combination of both—the problems you face are still the same. How do I create, market, and sell our products or services to the best of my ability? How do I hire, train, and keep the best employees to help us reach this goal? What is the best way to organize my company so it runs smoothly? How do I manage the money, the costs, the inventory, and the physical and psychological assets that make up our organization?

Amidst all of these questions come several important ones: How do I attract, serve, and keep customers? And if it's true that in business nothing happens until somebody sells something to somebody, it's even more true that no business can survive unless it directs all its efforts towards serving the people who ultimately do the buying—the customers. Unless the strategies, systems, and the service employees are centered on the needs and expectations of the customer, the organization will not thrive. It is time to turn your organization into a customer-focused entity and start *serving to succeed.*

Sometimes you have to stumble to prevent falling.

SERVICE BARRIERS

Not Understanding the Importance of Exceptional Customer Service

1. Sixty-eight percent of those customers who switch products and/or services do so because of the manner in which they were treated

2. Only 10% switch because of the dissatisfaction of the product and/or service

3. Taking care of the customer means taking care of business

4. The strength of the organization is dependent on customer service

5. The strength of customer service is dependent on continuous learning by the people who deliver it

Not Understanding The Customer Service Chain

1. In your position you are either dealing directly with the customer or with someone who does—chain reaction

2. Everyone in the organization impacts the customer service chain

3. Certain jobs or positions have the greatest opportunity to influence or retain customers

4. Everyone from the President and CEO to the Customer Service Representative has customers—if you're not serving the customer directly, serve someone who is

Not Understanding The Value Of A Customer

1. A customer is the most important person in any business

2. A customer is not dependent on us
3. A customer is the purpose of our work
4. A customer does us a favor when they do business with us
5. A customer is a person who brings us their needs
6. A customer makes it possible to pay our salaries
7. A customer is the life blood of any business

Not Understanding Why Customers Fire You

1. Showing no genuine or personal interest—impersonal service and insincere people
2. Poor response—some people will sacrifice quality for speed
3. Unavailability of people or product—when they can't get the stuff they need or reach the person they want, they'll go someplace else
4. Hard to conduct business or order—computer voice attendant rather than a real human being answers the phone
5. Unfriendly person on the front line—smile
6. Over-promising—when you over-promise and under-deliver, you lose
7. Poor professional package or image—customers want to feel that the quality of their business will be reflected by the quality of those they deal with

8. Nickel-and-diming—charging for incidentals such as copies, phone calls, and interest on late payments

9. Poor product quality—no matter how much people pay, they expect a quality product

10. Poor or rude collection practices—keeping the customer is as important as collecting the money

---

Enthusiasm makes everything different.

# # #

Service Culture

Mission

1. Who we are as an organization
2. What we are as an organization
3. Why we exist as an organization
4. Where we are headed as an organization
5. How we are going to get there as an organization

Values

1. Respect—treat everyone with dignity, and value different backgrounds, cultures, and viewpoints
2. Integrity—honesty, consistency, and professionalism in every facet of your behavior
3. Teamwork—work and communicate across functions, levels, geographies, and business units to build the organization; hold each other accountable for behavior and performance
4. Innovation—challenge yourselves by embracing innovation and creativity, not only in your products and services but also in all aspects of your work; learn from both your successes and failures
5. Quality—deliver the quality and craftsmanship that consumers demand

---

What you permit, you promote.

Objectives

1. Exceptional service—provide world-class service with personal concern for your customers and your team
2. Financial strength—to maintain a superior financial position and inspire the complete trust and confidence of your customers
3. Operational excellence—to deliver exceptional value to your customers through operational excellence
4. Unified team—to cultivate a highly motivated and committed team that embodies the organization's values
5. Innovative products and services—to meet your customers' needs
6. Market development—to develop and enhance the real and intrinsic long-term value of your customers

Customer-Focused

1. Leadership spends at least 20% of its time meeting with customers
2. Formal customer research is conducted at least once a year
3. Meetings with customers regularly involve people from several departments
4. Customers regularly rate you on service
5. Customer satisfaction is a key role in evaluating leadership performance
6. Management meetings devote as much time to customers' needs as they do to internal issues
7. Routinely partner with customers to solve problems
8. Staying in constant touch with customers rather than waiting until they have a problem

Defining Your Customer

Who Are Your Customers?

1. Existing customers—those who are doing business with you now

2. New customers—coming into contact with your organization for the first or second time

3. Potential customers—everyone who isn't your customer

   a. Advertising—direct mail

   b. Referrals—service excellence

   c. Location

   d. Price

   e. Accidentally or by chance

4. Internal customers—people who work in your organization and do business with each other

The Customer's Moments Of Truth

1. Moment of truth—first contact and first impression

2. Interim moments of truth—the service experience continues

3. Final moment of truth—the customer has completed business with you and is ready to grade the experience

---

Nothing happens without well-timed reminders.

The Customer's Outlook

1. Betrayed—once loyal but now committed to damaging your reputation

2. Angry—had a bad experience and now actively rejects you because they feel you owe them more than compensation

3. Disappointed—has no intention of working with you again and does not trust you

4. Stranger—has heard of you but has no opinion about you and what makes you different from the rest

5. Acquaintance—doing business with you but has no strong opinion and may only do business when the offer is good enough

6. Loyal—returns to you again and again, buys your latest products and/or services, and is willing to pay even more because of the service

7. Advocate—mentions you positively to friends and colleagues and will write a testimonial letter if you ask

8. Ambassador—actively promotes you by making introductions and enthusiastic recommendations

How Customers Impact Your Business

1. More transactions
2. More dollars per transaction

SERVICE GUIDELINES

Keep The Customer's Best Interest In Mind

1. Focus on your customer's needs and ask, "How can I help?" instead of "What can I sell?"
2. Ask questions to find out exactly what they need
    a. What types of issues are we facing?
    b. Can you describe what happened?
    c. What do you need in order to do this?
    d. If the customer knows what he or she needs, get it.
3. Give them what they want (need), not what you think they ought to have—no assuming and no forced agenda
4. Be honest with them about "wait times" such as appointments, shipments, and anything that requires them to wait for service
5. Don't be afraid to send them to the competition if the assessment warrants it
6. Watch out for them with regard to quantity, cost, and even the best way to ship your product

Serve Them By Using Your ACE

1. **A**ttentive to their requests
2. **C**aring about their needs
3. **E**xcited about your services and products

Earn The Right To Ask For More

1. Always confirm appointments—they appreciate the reminder

2. Develop a relationship before you address the customer's request or attempt to ask him or her for anything

3. Use the customer's name and encourage him or her to use yours—people always prefer to do business with someone they know

4. Replicate the very best experience you have ever had as a customer

5. See each customer as unique as you try to understand his or her needs, issues, and concerns

6. Look for opportunities to compliment the customer

7. Look for things you have in common with the customer

8. Be time sensitive—follow up when a deadline is involved

9. Throw in an extra—everyone likes to get more than expected

Work Hard To Keep Them

1. Contact each customer after the sale to ensure satisfaction with the product or service and verify that it was correct, on time, and in excellent condition

2. After you resolve a customer's problem, follow up to ensure everything is okay

3. Ask customers how they would like to be served and contacted, and give them a choice between phone, fax, or email

4. Send email and/or faxes each day notifying customers of their shipment and how it was shipped—tracking number if possible
5. Send a personalized thank-you note for their business with no agenda or purpose
6. Send handwritten notes to all key customers notifying them of special events or promotions

---

Problems provide the paycheck that customers sign.

# # #

SERVICE STRATEGIES

Build Solid Relationships

1. Give value: give value to customers, not facts about you
2. Tell truths: tell the truth even if it hurts or embarrasses you
3. Beat goals: customers are attracted to achievers
4. Gain knowledge: collect as much knowledge about customers as you do about your company and your product or service
5. Have answers: build your credibility as an information resource rather than as a salesperson
6. Tell stories: stories are personal, revealing, and help people relate
7. Tell how: what to do isn't as important as how to do it
8. Build value: gets customer's leads or put them in front of contacts that might lead them to business
9. Find links: find something in common that ties you together

---

Perspective is the way you see it, the way you want it, and the way it really is.

Focus On "What's Right"

1. View complaints as a second chance to impress customers

2. Never tell a customer what you *can't* do; their only interest is what you *can* do

3. The customer isn't always right, but it's never our job to prove the customer wrong

Be Unique In Your Approach

1. Dare to be different—risk success

2. Dare to try something new—risk failure

Practice The Five P's

1. Passion—love what you do, why you do it, and who you do it with

2. Prepared—you can claim to be surprised once; after that, you're unprepared

3. Polite—friendly and considerate no matter what kind of day you're having

4. Prompt—never keep a customer waiting without acknowledging them

5. Present—your customers want to be treated as individuals, not the next task

---

Become an expert in the impossible.

# # #

VALUE-ADDED SERVICE

Values That Have Nothing To Do With Price

1. Quality service to all customers
2. Product quality
3. Warranties or money-back guarantees
4. Service or installation after the sale
5. Industry leadership
6. Reputation for quality from satisfied customers
7. Reliability that extends through the company to products and services
8. Unique desire to do what is right for the customer every time

Follow Up

1. Current events—customer's locale
2. Industry information pertinent to their organization
3. Encouragement notes and cards
4. Logo items
5. Membership and rewards program
6. Direct telephone numbers
7. Celebrate service accomplishments—literature

Success is measured by your reaction to adversity.

Be Easy To Do Business With

1. Convenient business hours—survey your customers
2. Provide a service guarantee—if not met, give them something
3. Provide options—payment preference, shipping, ordering
4. Network luncheon for local customers
5. Frequent buyers club—discounts, gifts, free products
6. Customer directory—circulate and encourage customers to use
7. Take advantage of technology
   a. Phone system that has a provision to talk with someone
   b. Toll-free number
   c. After-hours answering system—return call the next day
   d. 24-hour emergency number
   e. Lose the music—benefit messages
   f. Utilize contact management software
   g. Utilize electronic greeting cards and newsletters
   h. Cyber network—bulletin board on your web site

Adversity is inevitable...misery is optional.

Feast On Customer Feedback

1. Email direct to owner/president
2. Customer advisory board—key clients that meet quarterly
3. Customer service survey—continue/stop/start

If you are not serving the customer, serve someone who is.

# # #

MASTERING YOUR MESSAGE

What Influences Your Message

1. Face-to-face communication
   a. Body language—55%
   b. Tone of voice—38%
   c. Words—7%
2. Telephone communication
   a. Tone of voice—82%
   b. Words—18%

Vocal Qualities

1. Tone—expresses feeling or emotion
2. Inflection—emphasizing words and syllables to enhance your message
3. Pitch—how high or deep your voice sounds
4. Rate—how many words spoken per minute
5. Volume—how loud or soft your voice sounds
6. Articulation—quality and clarity of words spoken

Life is tough...compared to what?

Phone Etiquette

1. Putting a caller on hold
   a. Explain why
   b. Ask permission
   c. Put the caller on hold
   d. Thank the caller for holding
2. Transferring a call
   a. Tell the caller to whom he or she will be transferred
   b. Explain why
   c. Ask permission
   d. Give the phone number and extension in case of disconnection
   e. Transfer the call

Ten Most Important Words To A Customer

1. Their own name
2. Yes
3. Thank you
4. Glad you're here
5. How may I serve you
6. What is most convenient for you
7. What else can I do for you
8. I'm not sure but I will find out
9. Thank you for your business—please come back again
10. I apologize for our mistake—let me make it right

#

HANDLING TOUGH CUSTOMERS

Prepare Yourself

1. View problems as opportunities
2. Be prepared to listen
3. See the customer's perspective first
4. Own the problem
5. Put the problem in context
6. Breathe

LEAP Into Resolution

1. **L**isten and let them vent
2. **E**ndure and stay calm
3. **A**cknowledge and mirror the customer's feelings
4. **P**amper their emotions and remain focused

A star shines the most when it is the darkest.

Don't Escalate The Situation

1. Never interrupt—listen first before you try to reason
2. Never argue—remember, your job is not to prove them wrong
3. Never assume—respect the customer's perceptions as real to him or her
4. Never quote your policies—some policies look better on paper than in practice

Action Steps

1. Accept responsibility—you are "they"
2. Take notes—focus on key points
3. Use "I" instead of "you"—"What can I do?" instead of "What do you need?"
4. Be agreeable—acknowledge their problem
5. Stay focused—your job is to meet the customer's needs

You must turn your back to the crowd in order for people to follow.

# # #

ONLINE SERVICE

Gaining The Customer's Trust

1. Total security
2. Only offer goods and services that are available
3. Over-communicate information to avoid unanswered questions
4. Be available 24/7
5. Build a system with seamless integration and user-friendly access

Meeting Customer Needs

1. Organize content to ease decision-making
2. Provide simple product and service descriptions
3. Facilitate various forms of contact
4. Support the product and services with inventory levels that guarantee fulfillment
5. Use an automated workflow tracking and strive for the lowest possible error rate
6. Make everything quick, pleasant, and effortless

Desire more than you can accomplish.

Email Procedures

1. Use software that prioritizes messages by date and lets the sender know the message has reached the proper department

2. Track the email questions you get and gear your answers to meet the specific needs of your customers

3. Provide links to let people pursue more detailed information

4. Offer recipients an easy way to unsubscribe with every electronic message you send

5. Make sure all outgoing email is useful, timely, and personalized

6. Never forget that email is a legal document

7. Train employees to convey an email message that keeps the human touch

Unfriendly Practices

1. Making it difficult for customers to navigate and find what they want

2. Treating customers anonymously

3. Teasing them with information that requires more detail

4. Designing a system without regard for customer needs

5. Making promises you can't deliver and being the answer to everything

6. Disregarding the coordination and sharing of information among various departments in the organization

PERFORMANCE MEASURES

Video Report Card

1. First impression—be smiling
2. Acknowledge customers immediately—100% attention
3. Customers awaiting a response—may I help the next person?
4. Tell them your name and use their name often
5. Sixty-second hold limit—give a status report
6. Don't transfer a call without an introduction of the caller
7. Body language—install mirrors for reflective behavior
8. Restate important information
9. Always thank a customer
10. Always invite them back

Service Habits

1. Greet the customer
2. Value the customer
3. Find out what the customer wants
4. Help the customer
5. Invite the customer back

**Men are from earth; women are from earth...
deal with it.**

Performance Indicators

1. Teamwork
2. Attitude
3. Customer service (internal and external)
4. Promoting company success

Critical Success Factors

1. Did I think of myself as a customer service professional today?

2. Did I maintain a positive attitude about my customers?

3. Did I provide excellent service to my internal customers and my company?

4. Did I work to build rapport and relationships with all my customers?

5. Was I able to ask good questions to better understand what my customers wanted?

6. Did I listen carefully to everything my customers said?

7. Was I able to offer more products, services, or options to my customers?

8. Did I handle complaints and difficult customers calmly and professionally?

9. Was I able to exceed my customers' expectations most of the time?

Enough white lies will make you go colorblind.

RECRUITING THE BEST

Top Ten Traits Of Customer Service Professionals

1. Optimism and enthusiasm
2. A positive mental image
3. A competitive spirit
4. A social disposition
5. An inquisitive mind
6. Organization
7. Respect
8. Accurate decision making
9. Communication
10. Knowledge

Characteristics Of An Effective Interview

1. Interviewee does 85% of the talking
2. Interviewer is assertive and engaging
3. Interviewer takes notes
4. Interviewer does not sell the position
5. Interviewer does not use the applicant's resume or job application to interview from
6. Interviewer probes desired qualities and behavior from a list of prepared questions

---

Self-improvement focus leaves no time for criticism.

Probing Principles

1. Ask general and ambiguous questions
2. Ask value judgment questions, not factual—what did you like least...?
3. Probe choice points and unusual situations—if you could have either...?
4. Ask questions unrelated to interviewee's experience or jobs

"Getting To Know You" Probes

1. If you could invite a well-known person to lunch, who would that be?
2. State an embarrassing moment in your life
3. What is your favorite book or Broadway play?
4. If you worked for you, what would be your number one constructive criticism?
5. Would winning one million dollars change your daily routine?
6. What would you like your legacy to be?

Always be learning.

# # #

Retaining The Best

Make The Right Impression First

1. What would impress you if you were a new employee?
2. What information would you want to have?
3. What information would you absolutely need?
4. Who would you like to meet?
5. What would make you feel like an accepted member of the team?

Creating A Better Workplace

1. Hire happy people—you ain't got enough time to teach happy
2. Provide a supportive work atmosphere—remove all threatening signs and turn "no" into a more gentle reminder
3. Ask them what they think—solicit regular feedback and reward the best idea of the month
4. Provide "I care" benefits—event tickets, AAA memberships, resources
5. Make people feel valuable—honor a different employee every week
6. Party—celebrate everything you can

I would rather be questioned for what I am, than believed for what I am not.

Elements To Ensure Employee Commitment

1. Balance between work and family life
2. Organizational direction
3. Growth opportunities
4. Recognition and rewards
5. Job satisfaction
6. Work environment

Growing Your Service Culture

1. Develop leadership—gain buy-in
2. Recruit the right people
3. Communicate the service vision
4. Provide continuous training
5. Establish sales and service goals
6. Monitor performance—what gets measured gets done
7. Reward performance—create incentive programs

Attitude doesn't solve problems, it only determines the outcome.

ADDITONAL PERSONAL GROWTH PRODUCTS
DEVELOPED BY STEVE GILLILAND
ARE AVAILABLE FROM

Performance Plus Professional Development, Inc.
1-877-499-8901

Founded in 1999 by Steve Gilliland, Performance Plus Professional Development is committed to increasing the effectiveness of people in all areas of life.

Through Performance Plus Professional Development, Steve Gilliland offers a wide range of training seminars, books, CDs, Videos, and DVDs designed to increase an individual's ability to influence and lead others.

A unique resource is Steve's bestselling book *Enjoy The Ride.* His philosophy centers on the simple premise that true success is not a thing you acquire or achieve. Rather, it is a journey you take your whole life long. Beginning with the compelling challenge to "check your passion," Steve ignites people's ability to choose what they do, why they do it, and who they do it with. In his refreshingly straight-forward style, Steve Gilliland shares unique insights into what it means to be successful. He enables readers to identify their dreams and puts genuine success within their reach. Add his humor and brilliant advantage of mixing words with wisdom, and Steve brings forth a book that truly motivates a reader to make changes and believe in the power of positive thinking.

To receive a catalog of resources available from Performance Plus Professional Development and additional information regarding Steve Gilliland's speaking itinerary, please call toll free 1-877-499-8901 or write:

Performance Plus Professional Development, Inc.
P.O. Box 4182
Pittsburgh, PA 15202

www.performanceplus1.com